The Shofar: The First Instrument of God's Voice
Copyright © 2012

Cover design by Jennifer Nelson

Compiled by Harlon L. Picker, Messianic Rabbi

Published by *JVMI Publishing,* a division of *Jewish Voice Ministries International*
P.O. Box 31998
Phoenix, Arizona 85046-1998
Phone: 602-971-8501
Fax: 602-971-6486
www.jewishvoice.org

ISBN #978-0-9821117-5-8

Printed in the United States of America

ACKNOWLEDGEMENTS

The Shofar was one of the things that first called me into Messianic Judaism. The first time I heard the sound of the Shofar I knew that the LORD (*ADONAI*) was calling me into an area of my life that had been long-since forgotten.

I come from an Orthodox Jewish family; both my paternal and maternal grandfathers were Rabbis. When my father's family immigrated to the United States in the 1890s to escape the pogroms in White Russia (Belarus) they kept to the strictest form of Judaism, Orthodox. My family moved to Tucson, Arizona in 1942 and started straying away from our Hebraic roots. By the time I was of age to go to Hebrew school in the 1960s, we had completely abandoned our faith. We still considered ourselves Jews because if you are born a Jew you will die a Jew.

It wasn't until 1997 when I met my wife, Joyce Rago, that I rediscovered my Jewish roots and identity as a Jewish Believer in the Messiah of Israel, Yeshua!

Joyce is my best friend and the love of my life. She has stood by me and helped me grow in my talents and abilities in all aspects of my life, but particularly in my walk with the LORD. Her profound influence helped direct me to answer the call of God on my life resulting in my becoming a Messianic Jewish Rabbi. Through her love and encouragement I have come to understand what the LORD has called me to do; she is the reason I am able to write this teaching at this point in my life. As my soul-mate and a Messianic Rabbi in her own right, she is the only one who could truly understand what it is that God is calling me to do with this teaching.

Another individual I would like to thank is Messianic Minister Christine Ashley. She sums up what I try to teach others about the importance of the *Sound of the Shofar*: "Excellence before the LORD is sounding His instrument." She is a true "Ba'al Tekiah" and my most excellent student. I have tried to pass this gift on to anyone who has been interested in the true meaning of the sound of the Shofar, and Christine has been a shining example of my life's work.

This booklet is meant to help all who are called to serve the God of Abraham, Isaac and Jacob understand what the Voice of God is saying to us. He wants us to be His Voice—His Shofar—to proclaim to a lost and dying world that Yeshua is the Messiah and the ONLY way to our Abba, our Father, in Heaven!

I hope this study will help you to understand the importance of God's Chosen Instrument and the true sound of His Voice. May it bless you and increase your understanding that we are ALL instruments of God and meant to be His Voice!

TABLE OF CONTENTS

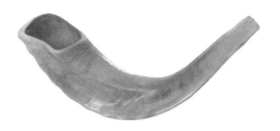

ORIGINS

Informational Overview of the Shofar and Its Origins

The **Shofar** is the ceremonial instrument of Judaism. It was not primarily used as a musical instrument. Its purpose had more to do with the making of an announcement or a proclamation of what was to follow. The Shofar is the only Hebrew cultural instrument to have survived until now. It is mainly used to worship *ADONAI* and to invoke His help during times of warfare.

According to the *Mishnah*, two different types of Shofarot were used in the Temple: one made of Ibex horn, its bell was ornamented with gold and was sounded at *Yom Teruah* (Rosh Hashanah) and during the *Yovel* (Jubilee) Days; and one made of ram's horn, its bell was ornamented with silver and was sounded on days of fasting.

We *sound* the Shofar, we do not *blow* it because it reminds us of the **Sound of God's Voice!**

The Shofar is generally a Ram's horn, but it can be from the horn of any kosher animal **except** a cow. (We don't want to remind God of the golden calf incident.) *Shofarot* (Shofars) are most often made from the horns of Big Horn Sheep, Goats, Ibex, Kudu, Oryx, Gazelle, or Antelope.

© Orin Zebest

http://listas.20minutos.es/lista/antilopes-253000/

There are two main types of Shofarot used today. The smaller one is commonly made from a Big Horn Sheep or Ram's horn and is very popular with *Ashkenazim* (Jews from German and Eastern European backgrounds). It produces a high, shrill sound.

9

The larger one is most often fashioned from the horn of an African Antelope called a Kudu and is popular with the *Sephardim* (Jews of Spanish and Portuguese backgrounds). It produces a low, ceremonial tone and is sometimes called a Yemenite horn.

There are two types of instruments in the *Tanakh* called *Shofarot* (Trumpets)—one is a Ram's horn and the other is a Silver Trumpet. The Silver Trumpet disappeared with the destruction of the second temple in 70 CE and the Yemenite horn has taken its place today.

In the Holy Temple, Silver Trumpets were used during the Divine service, as well as for announcing the arrival of the Shabbat, the New Moon, three of the biblical festivals; *Hag HaMatzah* (Unleavened Bread), *Shavu'ot* (Pentecost), *Sukkot* (Tabernacles), and for other various occasions.

The first time the Shofar is mentioned in the Scriptures is in Exodus 19:13:

> *"Not a hand shall touch him, but he shall surely be stoned or shot with an arrow; whether man or beast, he shall not live.' When the Shofar sounds long, they shall come near the mountain.'"*

The word *Shofar, Shofarot,* or *Ba'al Tekiah* is mentioned 124 times in the *Tanakh* and the *B'rit Chadashah* (see Appendix A—Biblical Scriptures on the Shofar).

God's voice is described as an Awesome Shofar blast in Hebrews 12:18-19:

> *"For you have not come to the mountain that may be touched and that burned with fire, and to blackness and darkness and tempest, and the sound of a Shofar and the voice of words, so that those who heard it begged that the word should not be spoken to them anymore."*

The Bible says that God's voice, or God himself will Sound the Shofar in ten (10) Scriptures.

In the Tanakh:
    Exodus 19:13, 16 & 19
    Exodus 20:18
    Isaiah 18:3
    Isaiah 27:13
    Zechariah 9:14

In the *B'rit Chadashah*:
    1 Thessalonians 4: 16
    Revelation 1:10 & 4:1.

1. Ibex
2. Oryx
3. Big Hom Sheep
4. Gazelle
Opposite page upper left: African Kudu

BIBLICAL OVERVIEW

BIBLICAL OVERVIEW OF THE SHOFAR'S USE AND DESIGN

As stated earlier, the Shofar is first mentioned in Exodus 19:13. It was sounded:

- *To proclaim the Jubilee Year and the proclamation of "freedom throughout the land" (Leviticus 25:9-10); this verse is engraved upon the Liberty Bell in Philadelphia, Pennsylvania*

- *On Rosh Hashanah, which is designated as "Yom Teruah" "A day of blowing" (Numbers 29:1)*

- *As an accompaniment to other musical instruments (Psalms 98:6)*

- *In processionals (Joshua 6:4)*

- *As a signal (Joshua 6:12, 2 Samuel 15:10)*

- *As a clarion call to war (Judges 3:27)*

- *To induce fear (Amos 3:6)*

The Shofar was or will be sounded for the following 16 reasons:

1 **To remind us of God's provision of a ram as a substitute for Isaac —** In Jewish tradition, the *Akedah* demonstrated God's *chesed*, His tender mercy toward His people, His justifying them solely on the merit of their confidence in His lovingkindness.

> *Genesis 22:13: Then Abraham lifted his eyes and looked, and there behind him was a ram caught in a thicket by its horns. So Abraham went and took the ram, and offered it up (or a burnt offering) instead of his son.*

2 **When the Torah was given to Israel as an instrument of proclamation, announcing the presence or coming of the LORD**

> *Exodus 19:19: And when the blast of the Shofar sounded long and became louder and louder, Moses spoke, and God answered him by voice.*

3 **To signal the sacred assembly of the Israelites**

> *Judges 3:27: And it happened, when he arrived, that he blew the Shofar in the mountains of Ephraim, and the children of Israel went down with him from the mountains; and he led them.*

4 To signal the assembly of the troops

Nehemiah 4:20: Wherever you hear the sound of the Shofar, rally to us there. Our God will fight for us.

5 As a warning

Numbers 10:9: When you go to war in your land against the enemy who oppresses you, then you shall sound an alarm with the trumpets (referring to the silver trumpets); and you will be remembered before the LORD your God, and you will be saved from your enemies.

6 In the midst of battle

Zechariah 9:14: Then the LORD will be seen over them, and His arrow will go forth like lightning. The LORD God will blow the Shofar, and go with whirlwinds from the south.

7 To remind us that God is sovereign

Psalm 47:5: God has gone up with a shout, the LORD with the sound of a Shofar.

8 To praise God

Psalm 98:6: With trumpets (referring to the silver trumpets) and the sound of a Shofar; shout joyfully before the LORD, the King.

9 To call God's people to worship Him

Isaiah 27:13: So it shall be in that day: The Great Shofar will be blown; they will come, who are about to perish in the land of Assyria, and they who are outcasts in the land of Egypt, and shall worship the LORD in the holy mount at Jerusalem.

10 As a call to repentance

Isaiah 58:1: Cry aloud, spare not; lift up your voice like a Shofar; tell My people their transgression, and the house of Jacob their sins.

11 Sounded over the offerings

2 Chronicles 29:26-29: The Levites stood with the instruments of David, and the priests with the trumpets. Then Hezekiah commanded them to offer the burnt offering on the altar. And when the burnt offering began, the song of the LORD also began, with the trumpets and with the instruments of David king of Israel. So all the assembly worshiped, the singers sang, and the trumpeters sounded; all this continued until the burnt offering was finished. And when they had finished offering, the king and all who were present with him bowed and worshiped.

12 At the swearing of an oath to God

2 Chronicles 15:14: Then they took an oath before the LORD with a loud voice, with shouting and trumpets (referring to the silver trumpets) and Shofarot.

13 To announce the beginning of the Year of Jubilee

Leviticus 25:9-10: Then you shall cause the trumpet of the Jubilee to sound on the tenth day of the seventh month; on the Day of Atonement you shall make the Shofar to sound throughout all your land. And you shall consecrate the fiftieth year, and proclaim liberty throughout all the land to all its inhabitants. It shall be a Jubilee for you; and each of you shall return to his possession, and each of you shall return to his family.

14 To usher in the Day of the LORD

Joel 2:1: Blow the Shofar in Zion, and sound an alarm in My holy mountain! Let all the inhabitants of the land tremble; for the day of the LORD is coming, for it is at hand.

15 At the resurrection of the dead and the return of Messiah Yeshua

1 Thessalonians 4:16-17: For the LORD Himself will descend from heaven with a shout, with the voice of an archangel, and with the Shofar of God. And the dead in Messiah will rise first. Then we who are alive and remain shall be caught up together with them in the clouds to meet the LORD in the air. And thus we shall always be with the LORD.

16 When God judges the earth

Revelation 1:10: I was in the Spirit on the Lord's Day, and I heard behind me a loud voice, as of a trumpet.

Rev 8:1-2, 6: When He opened the seventh seal, there was silence in heaven for about half an hour. And I saw the seven angels who stand before God, and to them were given seven Shofars . . . So the seven angels who had the seven Shofars prepared themselves to sound.

**NOTE: The Hebrew Gematria (numerical significance) of the number sixteen (16) means "love." The sound of the Shofar shows us the love that ADONAI (the LORD) has for his children. Halleluyah!

THE SHOFAR'S SIGNIFICANT SHAPE

The shape of the Shofar tells us something about how we must approach God.

- **When we look at a Shofar or Ram's Horn we see something very significant; it is rough, bent and twisted**

  It's rough exterior and crooked form depicts our growth as beings who are coarse and misshapen through life in a world plagued by sin. Though we are deformed, we have purpose. Sanctified by the atoning blood of Yeshua, our imperfect lives can become instruments of praise and glory.

- **Bent, bowed**

  As the Shofar, we bend and bow low before the LORD in homage and reverence.

- **In the harvesting of the Shofarot, the very strength and pride of the animal is removed; cut off. The animals are then penned and cared for because they are rendered helpless and unable to defend or protect themselves**

  When we approach God, our pride and the very essence of anything that would exalt itself over His place of authority in our lives must be removed until we are humbled and completely dependent upon Him.

We, too, must become broken before our LORD and King as we approach Him to hear His Voice!

Psalm 24:3-5: Who may ascend into the hill of the LORD? Or who may stand in His holy place? He who has clean hands and a pure heart, Who has not lifted up his soul to an idol, Nor sworn deceitfully. He shall receive blessing from the LORD, And righteousness from the God of his salvation.

Psalm 34:18-19: The LORD is near to those who have a broken heart, And saves such as have a contrite spirit. Many are the afflictions of the righteous, But the LORD delivers him out of them all.

Psalm 51:17: The sacrifices of God are a broken spirit, A broken and a contrite heart—These, O God, You will not despise.

Psalm 51:19: Then You shall be pleased with the sacrifices of righteousness, With burnt offering and whole burnt offering; Then they shall offer bulls on Your altar.

We cannot approach the LORD with a haughty or arrogant spirit. We must be humble and broken just like the sounds that come from the Shofar!

To be a true Ba'al Tekiah, we must be a humble instrument of the LORD!

Luke 20:18: "Whoever falls on that stone will be broken; but on whomever it falls, it will grind him to powder."

Isaiah 57:15: For thus says the High and Lofty One Who inhabits eternity, whose name is Holy: "I dwell in the high and holy place, With him who has a contrite and humble spirit, To revive the spirit of the humble, And to revive the heart of the contrite ones.

© Harlon Picker

SOUNDING THE SHOFAR

CALLS, SOUNDS,
PRACTICAL USE AND MAINTENANCE

THE CALLS AND SOUNDS OF THE SHOFAR

The Shofar has four basic calls that have been handed down throughout the ages. These terms can be found in the Scriptures at various points. The sequence we know today has been handed down as tradition. There were most likely other calls as well, but they have been lost over the centuries.

The calls for the Shofar can be likened to the calls that the bugler used during the period of mounted cavalry during the late 19th and earlier 20th centuries in U.S. history. When the commander would give a voice command, the bugler would give that command on the bugle so all the soldiers would know what to do. When our Commander, *ADONAI*, gives us a command, He either uses His voice, a Shofar or one of His angels to *"Sound the Shofar"* so we will know what He wants us to do!

The following are names and descriptions of the calls:

Tekiah—To Blow or Blast

A single medium length blast with a low-to-high pitch transition. Hard, short push on low pitch, slight sustain on high pitch, sometimes ended with a short, pushing, higher pitched burst. *Probably used at Jericho to bring the walls down (Joshua 6:5).*

Shevarim—Broken

Three blasts each low-to-high pitch sounded like triplets. Think of *Shevarim* as being three short *Tekiahs* without the short burst on the ends. *This could have been what was sounded as a call to repentance when the children of Israel sinned before ADONAI (Isaiah 58:1).*

Teruah—Battle Cry or Alarm

Teruah consists of rapid one-second pitch bursts in a staccato fashion. There should be nine or more bursts to make a *Teruah*. *Probably used by Gideon when they attacked the Midianites (Judges 7:22).*

Tekiah G'dollah—The Long or Great Blast

Similar to the *Tekiah*, only the high note is sustained for the longest possible breath. It is also ended with a violent, short, pushed-out breath of an even higher-pitched note. *Probably used at Mt. Sinai to assemble the Israelites (Exodus 19:19).*

May also be what is sounded when Messiah Yeshua returns (1 Thessalonians 4: 16).

It would have taken many calls and even series of calls to move three million Israelites around the desert (Judges 3:27).

There were undoubtedly calls that are not covered in this teaching. My research continues and I hope to find other calls which may have been used. In time, I believe *ADONAI* will unveil more answers that will help us to see an even clearer picture of how He used the sound of the Shofar to speak to His people.

HOW TO PLAY AND MAINTAIN YOUR SHOFAR

To play a Shofar properly, please observe the following steps:

1) Look at the mouthpiece. Shofar mouthpieces are usually irregular. If possible rotate the Shofar, positioning the thickest part of the mouthpiece in the upright position. This will make playing easier.

2) Place the mouthpiece against your lips. Use the very center of your lips. Traditional *Ba'al Tekiah* use the fleshy part of the lips to the left or to the right. This is a Rabbinic tradition and the Word of God *DOES NOT* specify how you are to sound the Shofar, just what it is that you will sound. Whichever method feels more comfortable to you is what you should use.

3) Take a deep breath, tighten and buzz your lips. (It's similar to a trumpet but requires a looser embouchure or lip position.)

4) Another exercise to strengthen your lips is to take the eraser end of a NEW pencil and place it between your lips. Tighten your lips around it by make a frown with your lips (corners of your mouth turned down). This will help you to develop your embouchure so that you can get the buzz sound you need to sound the Shofar. Do this exercise and hold the pencil with your lips until they ache. Rest and do this again for several minutes. As you strengthen your embouchure you will be able to raise and lower the pencil with your lips. By this time along with practicing buzzing with your lips you should be able to produce a wonderful sound with your Shofar.

5) Once you have produced a note, try to see what other notes you can obtain. If you will push your air-stream in an upwards direction, it will help you produce high notes more easily. The sound you will make with the back of your tongue will be ***aaah, eeeh and ickh*** to get a higher pitch as you tighten your lips.

6) Do not try to *over blow* the Shofar. If you cannot control your lips, putting more air through the Shofar will not make it easier to produce a note. It will cut off your sound altogether!

7) To get a long sustained blast, you must learn to breathe deeply using your diaphragm. Tighten up your abdomen muscles when playing.

Wind instrument players use parts of their lungs that most people never learn to use. Good posture also makes a great difference!

8) A great exercise to increase your abdomen muscles is to lie with your back against the floor. Place a heavy book such as a large dictionary or encyclopedia upon your abdomen. Practice breathing deeply so that you can move the book up and down with your breath, not your stomach muscles as you breathe. This will strengthen your abdomen muscles and give you the ability to hold your notes longer! As your abdomen strengthens, you can even add several books. Stomach crunches can also help to develop the proper breathing that a Ba'al Tekiah needs to hold a really long Tekiah G'dollah. An experienced Ba'al Tekiah (Master Blower or Sounder) can hold the Tekiah G'dollah for over one minute—now that takes breathe control. Circular breathing (*inhaling through your nose while exhaling through your mouth*) is NOT permitted while doing this.

Cleaning and Care of Your Shofar:

9) The Shofar must be cleaned regularly. Warm (not hot) soapy dish water in a bathtub works extremely well. A flexible wire trumpet brush does a great job on the inside and a washcloth will work well for the outside. After you have washed the Shofar, rinse it thoroughly with cool water. To help eliminate the odor that comes from the Shofar, I recommend the use of a dish sanitizer (similar to the kind used to sanitize glasses in restaurants). This will kill any bacteria that tends to grow on the inside of your Shofar. Bacteria is the main cause of Shofar odors. Follow the instructions on the package and mix with cool water. Allow the Shofar to sit in the water for ten (10) minutes. Remove and allow to air dry. If this procedure is followed on a regular basis, your Shofar will smell fresh. Apply some anointing oil, olive oil, or furniture polish to the outside of the Shofar and rub it in thoroughly with a soft, dry cloth. Hand buff with a cloth baby diaper until you have a natural sheen.

Clean your Shofar frequently if you use it regularly as bacteria grows quickly if not kept in check! You may want to put a few drops of anointing oil in the large end of the Shofar to help with the odors between cleanings. *NEVER* put anointing oil in the mouthpiece that your lips will touch.

10) According to Jewish tradition, a Shofar that becomes damaged or cracked cannot be repaired. It must be removed from service and buried. However, a cracked Shofar can be repaired using cyanoacrylate glue (Super Glue). The Gel type is preferable. Be careful to wait for it to dry. Fingernail repair kits can be useful in strengthening weak areas and applying repairs to Shofars. For major cracks you can even use fiberglass patch; similar to the kits used for a boat hull. If you have a significantly large crack, you should consider taking the Shofar out of service and purchase a new one.

11) Shofars should be kept in a tepid environment with controlled temperatures. Do not expose to extreme hot or cold temperatures (which means: do not leave it in your car). Shofars can deform in shape if exposed to hot, humid conditions. Sunlight will affect their appearance.

An Important Point To Remember:

12) Shofar Etiquette—The Shofar should not be played solely at the owner's discretion. Shofarot should mainly be played between songs during the praise and worship portion of the service.

There may be times when the Worship Leader will ask the Ba'al Tekim to play during a praise song. This would be the only time for an *inexperienced* player to play the Shofar *during* a Praise and Worship song. The Ba'al Tekiah may play as the *Ruach HaKodesh* (Holy Spirit) leads during a praise and worship song. But one must always be conscious of how the Ruach is moving in the service and careful *never* to disturb Him.

Shofars have different pitches depending on the length, thickness of the walls and the type of animal they have been harvested from. Keep pitch in mind if you wish to play with the worship song. I suggest consulting with your Worship Leader and trying your skill in practice to make sure you are not distracting others during worship. We must *ALWAYS* be sensitive to what the Ruach wants to do during our worship time!

© Erifyli Orli Tsavdari

THE SOUND OF GOD'S VOICE

HEARING GOD'S VOICE
IN THE CALL OF THE SHOFAR

The call of God to Abraham ...

Genesis (B'resheet) 22:1-14

> "Now it came to pass after these things that God tested Abraham, and
> said to him, "Abraham!" And he said, "Here I am." Then He said, "Take
> now your son, your only son Isaac, whom you love, and go to the land of
> Moriah, and offer him there as a burnt offering on one of the mountains of
> which I shall tell you."
>
> So Abraham rose early in the morning and saddled his donkey, and took
> two of his young men with him, and Isaac his son; and he split the wood
> for the burnt offering, and arose and went to the place of which God had
> told him. Then on the third day Abraham lifted his eyes and saw the place
> afar off. And Abraham said to his young men, "Stay here with the donkey;
> the lad and I will go yonder and worship, and we will come back to you."

> So Abraham took the
> wood of the burnt
> offering and laid it on
> Isaac his son; and he
> took the fire in his hand,
> and a knife, and the two
> of them went together.
> But Isaac spoke to
> Abraham his father and
> said, "My father!" And
> he said, "Here I am, my
> son." Then he said, "Look, the fire and the wood, but where is the lamb for a
> burnt offering?" And Abraham said, "My son, God will provide for Himself
> the lamb for a burnt offering."
>
> So the two of them went together. Then they came to the place of which
> God had told him. And Abraham built an altar there and placed the wood
> in order; and he bound Isaac his son and laid him on the altar, upon the
> wood. And Abraham stretched out his hand and took the knife to slay
> his son. But the Angel of the LORD called to him from heaven and said,
> "Abraham, Abraham!" So he said, "Here I am." And He said, "Do not lay
> your hand on the lad, or do anything to him; for now I know that you fear
> God, since you have not withheld your son, your only son, from Me."

Then Abraham lifted his eyes and looked, and there behind him was a ram caught in a thicket by its horns. So Abraham went and took the ram, and offered it up for a burnt offering instead of his son. And Abraham called the name of the place, The-LORD-Will-Provide; as it is said to this day, "In the Mount of The LORD it shall be provided."

When God called out to Abraham, he responded "Hineni" (Here am I). This is a response of total submission in the Hebrew language.

Strong's 2009 hinneh (hin-nay'); prolongation for 2005; lo!: KJV—behold, lo, see.

It literally means *"I am at your service LORD. What can I do for you?"* It is accompanied by one bowing in half to show reverence to the one that the word was directed to. Abraham was responding to God that he was in total submission to whatever He would request!

In verses 6 and 7, the word "wood" in the Hebrew actually means "tree."

Strong's 6086 *ets* (ates); from 6095; a tree (from its firmness); hence, wood (plural sticks): KJV—gallows, pine, plank, staff, stalk, stick, stock, timber, *tree*, wood.

The fact that Isaac was carrying a tree up to Mount Moriyah was in itself significant in the fact that he was going to be the sacrifice.

John 19:16-17: Then he delivered Him to them to be crucified. So they took Yeshua and led Him away. And He, bearing His cross, went out to a place called the Place of a Skull, which is called in Hebrew, Golgotha,

The word in Greek is—Strong's 4716 stauros (stow-ros); from the base of 2476; a stake or post (as set upright), i.e. (specifically) a pole or cross (as an instrument of capital punishment); figuratively, exposure to death, i.e. self-denial; by implication, the atonement of the Messiah: KJV—cross.

The fact that Isaac was carrying a "tree" up Mt. Moriyah, which is Golgotha, the same hill that Yeshua (Jesus) would be crucified on 2000 years later was even more significant.

When Abraham answered Isaac's question in verse 8 with the fact that "God Himself would provide the lamb for the burnt offering," he was speaking prophetically.

Exodus (Sh'mot) 12:21-23: Then Moses called for all the elders of Israel and said to them, 'Pick out and take lambs for yourselves according to your families, and kill the Passover lamb. And you shall take a bunch of hyssop, dip it in the blood that is in the basin, and strike the lintel and the two doorposts with the blood that is in the basin. And none of you shall go out of the door of his house until morning. For the LORD will pass through to strike the Egyptians; and when He sees the blood on the lintel and on the two doorposts, the LORD will pass over the door and not allow the destroyer to come into your houses to strike you.

The Exodus from Egypt would not take place for another 500 years. How did Abraham know that God Himself would provide a lamb for the sacrifice?

The Torah, God's instructions to the Israelites would not be given to His people for another 500 years. The only way that Abraham could know about using a lamb for a sacrifice was through the Ruach HaKodesh (The Holy Spirit of God).

In verse 13, Abraham looked up and saw a ram caught in a thicket by its horns. He would use this ram as a substitute sacrifice in place of his son Isaac. This would not be written about as an acceptable sacrifice until God gave the Torah to Moses some 500 years later!

THE GUILT OFFERING AND THE TWO TRUMPS

Every time we hear the ***"Voice of the Shofar,"*** it should remind us that God sent Yeshua as a *Substitute Sacrifice* for our sins. He is the one who died in our place!

The law of the guilt offering:

Leviticus (Vayikra) 5:17-19: "If a person sins, and commits any of these things which are forbidden to be done by the commandments of the LORD, though he does not know it, yet he is guilty and shall bear his iniquity. And he shall bring to the priest a ram without blemish from the flock, with your valuation, as a trespass offering. So the priest shall make atonement for him regarding his ignorance in which he erred and did not know it, and it shall be forgiven him. It is a trespass offering; he has certainly trespassed against the LORD.'

Did Abraham have a vision 2000 years into the future to see the Lamb of God that would take away the sins of the world?

John 1:29: The next day John saw Yeshua coming toward him, and said, "Behold! The Lamb of God who takes away the sin of the world!"

Yeshua told us that Abraham saw Him.

John 8:56-58: Your father Abraham rejoiced to see My day, and he saw it and was glad. Then the Jews said to Him, "You are not yet fifty years old, and have You seen Abraham?" Yeshua said to them, "Most assuredly, I say to you, before Abraham was, I AM (emphasis added)."

Abraham looked into the future and saw that God would provide Himself a sacrifice. Just as God provided a ram that day as a substitute sacrifice for Isaac, He would provide His Son as a lamb that would die in our place as our substitute sacrifice. ***Hallelu-Yah!***

In verse 14 we see that Abraham proclaimed that day that the LORD would provide. We know this phrase in English as *"Jehovah Jireh,"* but in Hebrew it is *"ADONAI Yireh,"* the LORD will see to it.

On the mountain of the LORD it will be provided. God provided His only begotten Son on the mountain of the LORD, Calvary (Golgotha) as atonement for the sins of man once and for all!

The horns of the ram that Abraham sacrificed would later be called Shofarot.

The Shofar is the ceremonial instrument of Judaism. It was not primarily used as a musical instrument. Its purpose had more to do with the making of an announcement or a proclamation of what was to follow. The Shofar is the only Hebrew cultural instrument to have survived until now. It is mainly used to worship *ADONAI* (The LORD) and to invoke His help during times of warfare. ***It is a horn of Power and Authority!***

There was a Jewish "legend" born out of the Genesis 22 story about Abraham and Isaac.

It says that God took the two horns from the ram that was sacrificed on Mt. Moriyah that day for use at a later time.

They would not be used by Abraham, but by the LORD Himself. One of the horns was blown by God at Mt. Sinai in Exodus 19. This was called the *Left Trump*. The story says that the *Right Trump* would be blown at the resurrection. We know from earlier in the booklet that the first time the word Shofar is used in the Word of God is in Exodus 19:13.

Something very significant happened in Exodus 19 that bears a closer look.

> *Exodus (Sh'mot) 19:16-20: Then it came to pass on the third day, in the morning, that there were thunderings and lightnings, and a thick cloud on the mountain; and the sound of the trumpet was very loud, so that all the people who were in the camp trembled. And Moses brought the people out of the camp to meet with God, and they stood at the foot of the mountain. Now Mount Sinai was completely in smoke, because the LORD descended upon it in fire. Its smoke ascended like the smoke of a furnace, and the whole mountain quaked greatly. And when the blast of the trumpet sounded long and became louder and louder, Moses spoke, and God answered him by voice. Then the LORD came down upon Mount Sinai, on the top of the mountain. And the LORD called Moses to the top of the mountain, and Moses went up.*

Why were the people frightened by the Voice of the Shofar? Because they knew that it was not Moses or any of the men of Israel sounding it. ***It was the Voice of God Himself!***

It says in verse 20 that God came down and Moses went up. There is one other place in the Word of God that talks about God coming down and someone going up. Remembering the Jewish "legend" of the ram's horns from Genesis 22 (on page 31), we will see a prophetic view in the following scripture of how the *Right Trump* will be sounded.

> *1 Thessalonians 4:16-17: For the Lord Himself will descend from heaven with a shout, with the voice of an archangel, and with the trumpet of God. And the dead in Christ will rise first. Then we who are alive and remain shall be caught up together with them in the clouds to meet the Lord in the air. And thus we shall always be with the Lord.*

God is going to use His Voice to call His people home! Baruch HaShem (Bless the Name)!

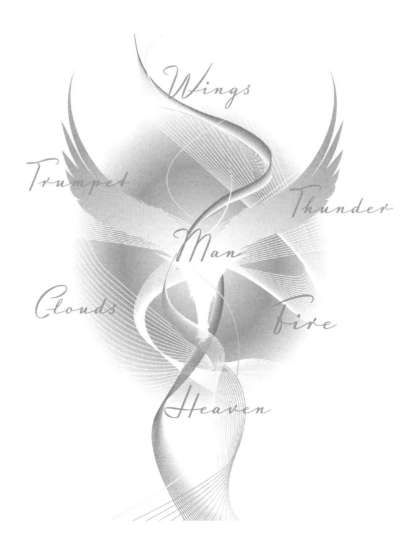

Wings

Trumpet

Thunder

Man

Clouds

Fire

Heaven

SEVEN OTHER SOUNDS OF GOD'S VOICE

God has given us the Shofar as a powerful tool to use in warfare against our adversary. It symbolizes the Sound of God's Voice.

When the Shofar is sounded, it may mean God is sending us physical help, spiritual help (Angels), or God Himself is coming to rescue us!!!

God's Voice can also be heard in these seven ways:

The Hebrew Gematria for the number seven (7) means completion or perfection.

1) Through the wings of the cherubim

Ezekiel 10:5: And the sound of the wings of the cherubim was heard even in the outer court, like the voice of Almighty God when He speaks.

2) Out of the fire

Deuteronomy 4:12: And the LORD spoke to you out of the midst of the fire. You heard the sound of the words, but saw no form; you only heard a voice.

3) Through the thunder

Job 40:9: Have you an arm like God? Or can you thunder with a voice like His?

4) With a voice from Heaven

Daniel 4:31: While the word was still in the king's mouth, a voice fell from heaven: "King Nebuchadnezzar, to you it is spoken: the kingdom has departed from you!

5) With a voice from a cloud

Mark 9:7: And a cloud came and overshadowed them; and a voice came out of the cloud, saying, "This is My beloved Son. Hear Him!"

6) With a voice like the sound of the trumpet

Hebrews 12:19: and the sound of a trumpet and the voice of words, so that those who heard it begged that the word should not be spoken to them anymore.

Revelation 1:10: I was in the Spirit on the Lord's Day, and I heard behind me a loud voice, as of a trumpet.

Revelation 4:1: After these things I looked, and behold, a door standing open in heaven. And the first voice which I heard was like a trumpet speaking with me, saying, "Come up here, and I will show you things which must take place after this."

7) Through the voice of man!

Genesis 1:27: So God created man in His own image; in the image of God He created him; male and female He created them.

Joshua 10:14: And there has been no day like that, before it or after it, that the LORD heeded the voice of a man; for the LORD fought for Israel.

You see today, whether you can sound the Shofar or not, **YOU ARE GOD'S VOICE!** Since we are made in God's image and likeness, as Believers in Messiah Yeshua we can command the blessings of God through our obedience to His Word and with our voice. Our voice IS the Voice of God when we are walking in obedience to Him.

John 14:13-14: And whatever you ask in My name, that I will do, that the Father may be glorified in the Son. If you ask anything in My name, I will do it.

John 15:16: You did not choose me, I chose you; and I have commissioned you to go and bear fruit, fruit that will last; so that whatever you ask from the Father in my name he may give you.

If we are Yeshua's, we know that He **IS** the Voice and the Image of God!

*John 15:15: No longer do I call you servants, for a servant does not know what his master is doing; but I have called you friends, for all things that **I heard** from My Father I have made known to you.*

*John 14:6-7: Jesus said to him, "I am the way, the truth, and the life. No one comes to the Father except through Me. **If you had known Me, you would have known My Father also; and from now on you know Him and have seen Him.**"*

We must always remember that when the Shofar is sounded, it is the sound of innocent blood. An innocent animal died to produce the Shofar. At one time innocent animals were killed so that people could use their horns as Shofarot. Today, the horns are "harvested" and the animals are left alive. We must keep in mind that horns are not like antlers, ***they never grow back!*** When the horns of an animal are taken to produce Shofarot, the animal is completely defenseless because its means of protection and defense have been stripped away.

We must understand that the Voice of God **IS** our protection and defense! If we try to survive in this world without God's protection, we will be defenseless just as the innocent animal is that gave up its horns to become Shofarot.

We also must understand that the Voice of God who became flesh and dwelt among us **IS** our defense. Yeshua is that Voice of God and it is He and He alone that is our defense!

Innocent blood was spilled and calls out to God whenever an animal gives of itself to be a sacrifice for our sins. Innocent blood has a voice. Remember the story of Cain and Abel? God asked Cain where his brother Abel was and Cain replied *"Am I my brother's keeper?"* God replied *"What have you done? Your brother's blood cries out to me from the ground."* We need to remember the substitute sacrifice that God sent to pay for our sins. His Son, Yeshua, is the One who died for our sins when His innocent blood was shed on Calvary.

You've heard the history of the Shofar and the calls. Now I want to give you two (famous) examples of what the Shofar can do when it is used for the Glory of God. ***God's Voice is a mighty instrument and will give us the victory!***

The Walls of Jericho

Joshua. 6:1-5: Now Jericho was securely shut up because of the children of Israel; none went out, and none came in. And the LORD said to Joshua: "See! I have given Jericho into your hand, its king, and the mighty men of valor. You shall march around the city, all you men of war; you shall go all around the city once. This you shall do six days. And seven priests shall bear seven trumpets of rams' horns before the ark. But the seventh day you shall march around the city seven times, and the priests shall blow the trumpets. **It shall come to pass, when they make a long blast with the ram's horn, and when you hear the sound of the trumpet, that all the people shall shout with a great shout; then the wall of the city will fall down flat. And the people shall go up every man straight before him."** *(Emphasis added)*

Gideon's Army

Judges 7:1-8: Then Jerubbaal (that is, Gideon) and all the people who were with him rose early and encamped beside the well of Harod, so that the camp of the Midianites was on the north side of them by the hill of Moreh in the valley. And the LORD said to Gideon, "The people who are with you are too many for Me to give the Midianites into their hands, lest Israel claim glory for itself against Me, saying, 'My own hand has saved me: Now therefore, proclaim in the hearing of the people, saying, 'Whoever is fearful and afraid, let him turn and depart at once from Mount Gilead.'"

And twenty-two thousand of the people returned, and ten thousand remained. But the LORD said to Gideon, "The people are still too many; bring them down to the water, and I will test them for you there. Then it will be, that of whom I say to you, 'This one shall go with you,' the same shall go with you; and of whomever I say to you, 'This one shall not go with you,' the same shall not go."

So he brought the people down to the water. And the LORD said to Gideon, "Everyone who laps from the water with his tongue, as a dog laps, you shall set apart by himself; likewise everyone who gets down on his knees to drink.' And the number of those who lapped, putting their hand to their mouth, was three hundred men; but all the rest of the people got down on their knees to drink water.

Then the LORD said to Gideon, "By the three hundred men who lapped I will save you, and deliver the Midianites into your hand. Let all the other people go, every man to his place." So the people took provisions and their trumpets in their hands. And he sent away all the rest of Israel, every man to his tent, and retained those three hundred men. Now the camp of Midian was below him in the valley.

Judges 7:16-22: Then he divided the three hundred men into three companies, and he put a trumpet into every man's hand, with empty pitchers, and torches inside the pitchers. And he said to them, "Look at me and do likewise; watch, and when I come to the edge of the camp you shall do as I do: When I blow the trumpet, I and all who are with me, then you also blow the trumpets on every side of the whole camp, and say, 'The sword of the LORD and of Gideon!'"

So Gideon and the hundred men who were with him came to the outpost of the camp at the beginning of the middle watch, just as they had posted the watch; and they blew the trumpets and broke the pitchers that were in their hands. Then the three companies blew the trumpets and broke the pitchers—they held the torches in their left hands and the trumpets in their right hands for blowing—and they cried, "The sword of the LORD and of Gideon!" And every man stood in his place all around the camp; and the whole army ran and cried out and fled.

When the three hundred blew the trumpets, the LORD set every man's sword against his companion throughout the whole camp; and the army fled to Beth Acacia, toward Zererah, as far as the border of Ahel Meholah, by Tabbath. *(Emphasis added)*

The call of the Shofar should be used just as prayer and fasting is used when we beseech God for answers to the issues of life. Just as we use our voices to cry out to our LORD, we can also use the Shofar to cry out to the LORD.

The Shofar is a weapon of war! To the adversary; the sound symbolizes the power of our God; the God of Abraham, Isaac and Jacob! When we sound the Shofar we scatter and confuse the enemy. The enemy cannot tell whether it is a man, an angel, or God's Voice itself. Satan cannot take the chance that it's not God's Voice!

One day soon, we will once again hear the Sound of the Shofar and know that God's promises are coming to pass as He sends His Son Yeshua to come for His bride.

Make preparation, ready-or-not, here He comes! Are you ready to hear the "Sound of the Shofar?"

shutterstock/ Arkady Mazor

THE SHOFAR IN TALMUDIC HISTORY

HISTORICAL ACCOUNTS, BLESSINGS, AND HOLY DAY TRADITIONS

TALMUDIC HISTORY OF THE SHOFAR

When used in the Temple, the Shofar was generally sounded in conjunction with the trumpet (*hazozrah*). The *Talmud* (RH 27a) states that the trumpet was made of silver while the processed horn of one of the five species of animal—Sheep, Goat, Big Horn Sheep, Antelope, and Gazelle— was used to fulfill the ritual commandment of the sounding of the Shofar. It further declares (ibid. 26b) that the Shofar should preferably be made of a ram's or wild goat's horn, because they are curved. Rabbi Judah states:

> *"the Shofar of Rosh Hashanah (Yom Teruah) must be of the horn of a ram, to indicate submission."*

Traditionally a ram's horn is sounded on those days because of its connection with the sacrifice of Isaac (known as the Akedah), which is contained in the Torah reading for the second day of the festival. Conversely, a cow's horn may not be used because of the incident of the golden calf (RH 3:2). The Shofar may not be painted, though it may be gilded or carved with artistic designs, while the mouthpiece must remain natural. A Shofar with a hole is deemed halakhically unfit, though it may be used if no other is available (Sh. Ar., OH 586). **The Talmud states that the Shofar is blasted in order to frighten and confound Satan.**

Use on the Holy Days

During the month of Elul, the Shofar is blown from the second day of the new month to usher in the penitential season (Rema, Sh. Ar., OH 581:1).

There is a tradition that Moses ascended Mount Sinai for the second time on Rosh Chodesh Elul and that **the Shofar was sounded so that the children of Israel might not be misled.** Thus, originally it was blown only on the first day of Rosh Chodesh Elul. Today it is sounded daily, except for the last day, throughout the month at morning service until Yom Teruah is over, and once more on the Day of Atonement at the conclusion of the final service (Ne'ilah). This last sounding, however, is a late custom.

On Yom Teruah, Psalm 47 is recited seven times before the sounding of the Shofar. This is symbolic of the seven circuits that the Israelites made around Jericho before the wall fell down at the blasts of the Shofar, and of the seven heavens through which prayers must penetrate in order to reach the throne of God.

Psalm 47:1-9: To the Chief Musician. A Psalm of the sons of Korah.

Oh, clap your hands, all you peoples! Shout to God with the voice of triumph! For the LORD Most High is awesome; He is a great King over all the earth. He will subdue the peoples under us, and the nations under our feet. He will choose our inheritance for us, the excellence of Jacob whom He loves. Selah

God has gone up with a shout, the LORD with the sound of a trumpet. Sing praises to God, sing praises! Sing praises to our King, sing praises! For God is the King of all the earth; sing praises with understanding. God reigns over the nations; God sits on His holy throne. The princes of the people have gathered together, the people of the God of Abraham. For the shields of the earth belong to God; He is greatly exalted.

There are two series of blasts:

1. The *teki'ot meyushav* (*"sitting" teki'ot*), is sounded before the *Musaf.* The congregation rises from their seats to hear it.

2. The second series of blasts is sounded during the *Musaf Amidah*, while the congregation is standing.

This first series is preceded by two benedictions:

1) *Baruch atah, Adonai elohainu, melech haolam, ashair keedshanu bimetzvotav vtzevanu leeshmoah kol shofar.*

בָּרוּךְ אַתָּה יְהוָה אֱלֹהֵינוּ מֶלֶךְ הָעוֹלָם. אֲשֶׁר קִדְּשָׁנוּ בְּמִצְוֹתָיו, וְצִוָּנוּ לִשְׁמֹעַ קוֹל שׁוֹפָר

Blessed are You, O LORD our God, King of the universe, who makes us holy with mitzvot and calls us to hear the sound of the shofar.

2) *Baruch atah, Adonai elohainu, melech haolam, shehecheyanu vikeemanu v'heegeanu lozzmon hazeh.*

בָּרוּךְ אַתָּה יְהוָה אֱלֹהֵינוּ מֶלֶךְ הָעוֹלָם. שֶׁהֶחֱיָנוּ וְקִיְּמָנוּ וְהִגִּיעָנוּ לַזְּמַן הַזֶּה.

Blessed are You, O LORD our God, King of the universe, for giving us life, for sustaining us, and for enabling us to reach this season.

The second series, the *teki'ot me'ummad* ("standing *teki'ot*") is heard three times during the reader's repetition of the Musaf (in the Sephardim rite also in the silent Amidah) at the conclusion of each one of its major sections (*Malkhuyyot*—the kingship of God; *Zikhronot*-the remembrance of the merit of our ancestors; and Shofarot—hope for the coming of the Messianic Era to be ushered in by the sound of the Shofar). In some communities it is also customary to sound up to a total of one hundred sounds at the conclusion of the service.

The Shofar may be sounded only in the daytime. Women and children are exempt from the commandment to listen to it, but such is its place in the Yom Teruah ritual that nearly all do. When Yom Teruah occurs on the Sabbath, the Shofar is not blown, the traditional reason being "lest he carry it (the Shofar) from one domain to another (in violation of the Sabbath)" (RH 29b). When the Temple was in existence it was sounded there even on the Sabbath, but not elsewhere. After the destruction of the Temple Johanan b. Zakkai permitted its use on the Sabbath in a town where an ordained *bet din* sat (RH 4:1). This, however, is not the standard practice in our times. The congregant sounding the Shofar is called a *Ba'al Teki'ah* and anyone capable of doing so is permitted to blow it. The prompter, or caller, is the *Makri*.

Maimonides gives a moving interpretation of the sounding of the Shofar:

'Awake O sleepers from your sleep, O slumberers arouse ye from your slumbers, and examine your deeds, return in repentance and remember your Creator" (Yad, Teshuvah 3:4).

We learn from the Mishnah and the Talmud that in the Hellenistic period no improvements or modifications that might affect the tone were permitted; no gold-plating on its interior, no plugging of holes, no alteration of its length (the minimum permissible length of a ritually approved Shofar was three (3) handbreadths); the Shofar tone was to be preserved unaltered. Nor was the process of steaming or boiling permitted.

On Yom Teruah you can sound a short version of what is sounded in the temple service.

It consists of the following calls:

Tekiah, Shevarim, Teruah, Tekiah

Tekiah, Shevarim, Tekiah

Tekiah, Teruah, Tekiah

Tekiah G'dollah

The full version of the 100 Shofar Calls for Yom Teruah are as follows:

Makri to recite:

Tekiah, Shevarim, Teruah, Tekiah

Tekiah, Shevarim, Teruah, Tekiah

Tekiah, Shevarim, Teruah, Tekiah

Tekiah, Shevarim, Tekiah

Tekiah, Shevarim, Tekiah

Tekiah, Shevarim, Tekiah

Tekiah, Teruah, Tekiah

Tekiah, Teruah, Tekiah

Tekiah, Teruah, Tekiah G'dollah

Malkhuyyot—this emphasizes God's Majesty and His lofty position as Sovereign King of the universe.

"May all the inhabitants of the world realize and know that to you, every knee must bend, every tongue must vow allegiance . . . The LORD *shall be King forever and ever."*

Makri to recite:

Tekiah, Shevarim, Teruah, Tekiah

Tekiah, Shavarim, Tekiah

Tekiah, Teruah, Tekiah

Zikhronot—testifies of God's remembrance of His everlasting covenant with Israel.

"Remember on our behalf, LORD *our God, the covenant, the kindness, and the solemn promise which you did make to our father Avraham on Mount Moriyah."*

Makri to recite:

Tekiah, Shevarim, Teruah, Tekiah

Tekiah, Shevarim, Tekiah

Tekiah, Teruah, Tekiah

Shofarot—focuses upon the key role of the Shofar in the history of the nation. It speaks of Mt. Sinai where the LORD first revealed Himself with the sound of the Shofar. It reminds us of the coming of the Messianic Era to be ushered in by the sound of the Shofar.

"The whole world trembled at your presence, creation shook in awe before you, when you, our King, did reveal yourself on Mount Sinai . . . Amid the blasting of the Shofar did you appear to them."

Makri to recite:

Tekiah, Shevarim, Teruah, Tekiah

Tekiah, Shavarim, Tekiah

Tekiah, Teruah, Tekiah

The following seven sentences are quotations from the Psalms and Lamentations:

Psalm 118:5: I called on the LORD in distress; the LORD answered me and set me in a broad place.

Lamentations 3:56: You have heard my voice: "Do not hide Your ear from my sighing, from my cry for help.

Psalm 119:160: The entirety of Your word is truth, and every one of Your righteous judgments endures forever.

Psalm 119:133: Direct my steps by Your word, and let no iniquity have dominion over me.

Psalm 119:162: I rejoice at Your word as one who finds great treasure.

Psalm 119:66: Teach me good judgment and knowledge, for I believe Your commandments.

Psalm 119:108: Accept, I pray, the freewill offerings of my mouth, O LORD, and teach me Your judgments.

Makri to recite:

Tekiah, Shavarim, Teruah, Tekiah

Tekiah, Shevarim, Teruah, Tekiah

Tekiah, Shavarim, Teruah, Tekiah

Tekiah, Shevarim, Tekiah

Tekiah, Shavarim, Tekiah

Tekiah, Shevarim, Tekiah

Tekiah, Teruah, Tekiah

Tekiah, Teruah, Tekiah

Tekiah, Teruah, Tekiah G'dollah

Rabbi Moses Maimonides gives a moving interpretation of the sounding of the Shofar:

'Awake O sleepers from your sleep, O slumberers arouse ye from your slumbers, and examine your deeds, return in repentance and remember your Creator" (Yad, Teshuvah 3:4).

Makri to recite:

Tekiah, Shavarim, Teruah, Tekiah

Tekiah, Shevarim, Tekiah

Tekiah, Teruah, Tekiah G'dollah

In a spiritual sense, the sequence in which the Shofar calls are blown symbolizes the fall of mankind. It reminds us of our sinful nature and that we need a savior and His blood sacrifice to make us whole again. The final call that is blown is encouraging as it announces to us that the broken world is made whole again.

Each series of Shofar blasts begins and ends with a Tekiah (the long continuous note). These are like parentheses to the broken blasts that are sounded in between. This echoes the theme of Yom Teruah, "We were whole, we became broken, but we shall be whole again." And by the blood of Yeshua, we are!

This word *shout* uses the same verbal root as "Teruah." The word "Teruah" can indicate various methods of noisemaking from shouting in prayer to blowing on the Silver Trumpets. All of these the Tanakh (Old Covenant) describes as acts of worshipping the LORD. Psalm 150 sums up how to Praise the LORD!

> *Ps 150:1-6: Halleluyah! Praise God in his holy place! Praise him in the heavenly dome of his power! Praise him for his mighty deeds! Praise him for his surpassing greatness! Praise him with a blast on the shofar! Praise him with lute and lyre! Praise him with tambourines and dancing! Praise him with flutes and strings! Praise him with clanging cymbals! Praise him with loud crashing cymbals! Let everything that has breath praise ADONAI! Halleluyah!*

Any way you look at it, God is to be praised with "Teruah" (Shout).

Here is more Rabbinic interpretation for the sounds of the Shofar on Yom Teruah and Yom Kippur. The writer is the founder and chancellor of Ohr Torah Stone Colleges and Graduate Programs, and chief rabbi of Efrat.

> *"Yom Teruah is "the day of the sounding of the Shofar [ram's horn],"* *according to its biblical definition (Numbers 29:1). However, Yom* *Kippur, the Day of Atonement and Forgiveness, likewise involves Shofar* *blasts following the poignant ne'ila (closing) prayer and generally* *serving as the conclusion of the fast.*
>
> *What is the biblical basis—if any—for the Shofar sound on Yom Kippur, and how does it differ from the Shofar on Yom Teruah?*
>
> *Let us first explore the significance of the Yom Teruah Shofar.*
>
> *Fascinatingly, the sages of the Talmud teach that the biblical "day of the sound of the Shofar" refers to the straight (tekiah), broken (shevarim, teruah) and straight ram's horn blasts linked to the musaf amida (additional standing prayer). Indeed, the initial custom was to sound the Shofar even during the silent amida—something still done in most Sephardi and Hassidic synagogues, but considered too confusing for most Ashkenazim (B. T. Rosh Hashana 33). Logic would dictate that if the shofar blasts*

are not considered an "interruption" (*hafsaka*) of the amida prayer, they must be seen as a part of the prayer. And so Rabbi Joseph B. Soloveitchik explains the true significance of the Shofar sounds (based on the rulings of Maimonides and the explication of Rabbi Haim Brisker) as prayer by means of sounds.

We pray with words—the verbal formulations of God's Kingship (Malkhuyyot), God's Remembrances (Zikhronot) and God's Rams horn blasts (Shofarot)—and we pray with sounds: the exultant, victorious *tekiah* shout, the sighing and sobbing *shevarim-teruah* cries, and the concluding, victorious *tekiah* once again for final emphasis.

The crafted verbal formulation interconnected with the primal Shofar sounds provide a powerful message: God is King not only of Israel but of the entire world; there is an architect to creation, and life is not "a tale told by an idiot, filled with sound and fury, signifying nothing." But if God is truly King, then He can rightfully hold us mortals accountable—especially for the fact that His ethical monotheism has not yet been accepted by the world, and not even by the majority of Israel. Hence we express sighs and sobs at our failings. We nevertheless conclude with an exultant shout, since repentance holds out the possibility of forgiveness, reconstruction and repair.

The same is true regarding remembrances. The axiom that there is also a divine plan for history, with a specific function set aside for nations as well as individuals, deserves an exultant shout, engendered by the knowledge that there is a more perfect society toward which we are heading; however, it also occasions sighs and sobs, lest we are not successfully fulfilling our mission, lest we are on the wrong track, in the wrong ball-park. And finally Shofarot, the Ram's Horn blast which emanated from atop Mount Sinai at the time of the Revelation.

Here too, we express the consummate joy of the *tekiah* with the realization that God has given us His Torah, His formula for a proper and satisfying moral, ethical and spiritual life, which we must learn ourselves and then communicate to the world. Herein lies the means through which we can become a "holy nation and a kingdom of priest-teachers." However, the sighs and sobs emanate from the fact that we ourselves are often found wanting; how can we teach others what we ourselves have failed to learn? In all these instances, the sound of the Shofar is the sound of the Jew, a primal sound emanating from the most essential inner "divine portion," his exultant prayer of gratitude and his beseeching request for strength and discipline to fulfill his mission. Indeed, we pray with words and sounds.

However, there is one crucial difference between the first two instances of Malkhuyyot and Zikhronot wherein the sounds emanate from the individual at prayer—and Shofarot, wherein the sound initially emanated from God: "God rose up through the sound of the teruah, the LORD was in the sound of the Shofar." Similarly, at the time of the redemption "all the inhabitants of the world and the dwellers on earth will see, when the banner on the mountains is held aloft; and they will all hear, when [God] will blast the Shofar" (Isaiah 18:3), and then again, "And it will happen on that day that the great Shofar shall be sounded [by God], and those who are lost in the land of Assyria and scattered in the land of Egypt shall come up and bow down before the LORD on the holy mountain in Jerusalem" (Isaiah 18:30).

Now we can begin to see the difference: the Shofar blast on Yom Kippur is not derived from the biblical "day of the broken, staccato sound which is unto you," because the biblical text there relates to the people ("unto you") who are sounding the Shofar at prayer, and since on Yom Teruah the major emotion on this first of the Ten Days of Repentance is that of inadequacy, sighing and sobbing, teruah, the very day is biblically defined as a "day of teruah."

The Shofar blast on Yom Kippur, on the other hand, is derived from the straight and exultant tekiah of Yom Kippur on the Jubilee year, the majestic declaration of "freedom throughout the land," the glorious announcement of redemption. (Leviticus 25:9-11, utilizing the Hebrew word Shofar, signifying a beautiful, joyous straight sound.) This is proper for Yom Kippur, the day when God promises—and guarantees—forgiveness and purification after five prayers in which we affirm (and request) that our Temple be a House of Prayer far all nations. And even though the Yom Kippur blast nowadays is only a rabbinical reminder of the Jubilee, every traditional Jew awaits the final blast by God, with its inherent vision of universal Revelation—when "He will enable us to hear again before the eyes of all living beings"—the redemptive Shofar call to the entire world in the days of the Messiah."

APPENDICES

The following **124 Scriptures** refer to the Shofar (Trumpet) from the Tanakh (Old Covenant) to the B'rit Chadashah (New Covenant). **Denotes God Himself or His Voice.

Shofar (Trumpet or Horn)

Exodus 19:13**: *Not a hand shall touch him, but he shall surely be stoned or shot with an arrow; whether man or beast, he shall not live.' When the **trumpet** sounds long, they shall come near the mountain."*

Exodus19:16**: *Then it came to pass on the third day, in the morning, that there were thunderings and lightnings, and a thick cloud on the mountain; and the sound of the **trumpet** was very loud, so that all the people who were in the camp trembled.*

Exodus19:19**: *And when the blast of the **trumpet** sounded long and became louder and louder, Moses spoke, and God answered him by voice.*

Exodus 20:18**: *Now all the people witnessed the thunderings, the lightning flashes, the sound of the **trumpet**, and the mountain smoking; and when the people saw it, they trembled and stood afar off.*

Leviticus 25:9 *(2 references):* *Then you shall cause the **trumpet** of the Jubilee to sound on the tenth day of the seventh month; on the Day of Atonement you shall make the **trumpet** to sound throughout all your land.*

Joshua 6:5 *(2 references—ram's horn and trumpet):* *It shall come to pass, when they make a long blast with the **ram's horn**, and when you hear the sound of the **trumpet**, that all the people shall shout with a great shout; then the wall of the city will fall down flat. And the people shall go up every man straight before him.'*

Judges 3:27: *And it happened, when he arrived, that he blew the **trumpet** in the mountains of Ephraim, and the children of Israel went down with him from the mountains; and he led them.*

Judges 6:34: *But the Spirit of the LORD came upon Gideon; then he blew the **trumpet**, and the Abiezrites gathered behind him.*

Judges 7:16: *Then he divided the three hundred men into three companies, and he put a **trumpet** into every man's hand, with empty pitchers, and torches inside the pitchers.*

Judges 7:18 (2 references—trumpet and trumpets): *When I blow the* **trumpet***, I and all who are with me, then you also blow the* **trumpets** *on every side of the whole camp, and say, "The sword of the LORD and of Gideon!' "*

I Samuel 13:3: And Jonathan attacked the garrison of the Philistines that was in Geba, and the Philistines heard of it. Then Saul blew the **trumpet** *throughout all the land, saying, "Let the Hebrews hear!"*

II Samuel 2:28: So Joab blew a **trumpet***; and all the people stood still and did not pursue Israel anymore, nor did they fight anymore.*

II Samuel 6:15: So David and all the house of Israel brought up the ark of the LORD with shouting and with the sound of the **trumpet***.*

II Samuel 15:10: Then Absalom sent spies throughout all the tribes of Israel, saying, "As soon as you hear the sound of the **trumpet***, then you shall say, 'Absalom reigns in Hebron!' "*

II Samuel 18:16: So Joab blew the **trumpet***, and the people returned from pursuing Israel. For Joab held back the people.*

II Samuel 20:16: So Joab blew the **trumpet***, and the people returned from pursuing Israel. For Joab held back the people.*

II Samuel 20:22: Then the woman in her wisdom went to all the people. And they cut off the head of Sheba the son of Bichri, and threw it out to Joab. Then he blew a **trumpet***, and they withdrew from the city, every man to his tent. So Joab returned to the king at Jerusalem.*

I Kings 1:34: There let Zadok the priest and Nathan the prophet anoint him king over Israel; and blow the **horn***, and say, 'Long live King Solomon!'*

I Kings 1:39: Then Zadok the priest took a horn of oil from the tabernacle and anointed Solomon. And they blew the **horn***, and all the people said, "Long live King Solomon!"*

I Kings 1:41: Now Adonijah and all the guests who were with him heard it as they finished eating. And when Joab heard the sound of the **horn***, he said, "Why is the city in such a noisy uproar?"*

Nehemiah 4:18: Every one of the builders had his sword girded at his side as he built. And the one who sounded the **trumpet** *was beside me.*

Nehemiah 4:20: Wherever you hear the sound of the **trumpet***, rally to us there. Our God will fight for us.'*

Job 39:24: *He devours the distance with fierceness and rage; Nor does he come to a halt because the **trumpet** has sounded.*

Job 39:25: *At the blast of the **trumpet** he says, 'Aha!' He smells the battle from afar, the thunder of captains and shouting.*

Psalm 47:5: *God has gone up with a shout, the LORD with the sound of a **trumpet**.*

Psalm 81:3: *Blow the **trumpet** at the time of the New Moon, at the full moon, on our solemn feast day.*

Psalm 150:3: *Praise Him with the sound of the **trumpet**; praise Him with the lute and harp!*

Isaiah 18:3**: *All inhabitants of the world and dwellers on the earth: when he lifts up a banner on the mountains, you see it; and when he blows a **trumpet**, you hear it.*

Isaiah 27:13**: *So it shall be in that day: the great **trumpet** will be blown; they will come, who are about to perish in the land of Assyria, and they who are outcasts in the land of Egypt, and shall worship the LORD in the holy mount at Jerusalem.*

Isaiah 58:1: *Cry aloud, spare not; lift up your voice like a **trumpet**; tell My people their transgression, and the house of Jacob their sins.*

Jeremiah 4:5: *Declare in Judah and proclaim in Jerusalem, and say: "Blow the **trumpet** in the land; cry, 'gather together,' and say, 'Assemble yourselves, and let us go into the fortified cities.'*

Jeremiah 4:19: *O my soul, my soul! I am pained in my very heart! My heart makes a noise in me; I cannot hold my peace. Because you have heard, O my soul, the sound of the **trumpet**, the alarm of war.*

Jeremiah 4:21: *How long will I see the standard, and hear the sound of the **trumpet**?*

Jeremiah 6:1: *O you children of Benjamin, gather yourselves to flee from the midst of Jerusalem! Blow the **trumpet** in Tekoa, and set up a signal-fire in Beth Haccerem; for disaster appears out of the north, and great destruction.*

Jeremiah 6:17: *Also, I set watchmen over you, saying, 'Listen to the sound of the **trumpet**!' But they said, 'We will not listen.'*

Jeremiah 42:14: *saying, 'No, but we will go to the land of Egypt where we shall see no war, nor hear the sound of the **trumpet**, nor be hungry for bread, and there we will dwell'*

Jeremiah 51:27: Set up a banner in the land, blow the **trumpet** among the nations! Prepare the nations against her, call the kingdoms together against her: Ararat, Minni, and Ashkenaz. Appoint a general against her; cause the horses to come up like the bristling locusts.

Ezekiel 17:14: "They have blown the **trumpet** and made everyone ready, but no one goes to battle; for My wrath is on all their multitude.

Ezekiel 33:3, 4, 5, 6 (4 references): when he sees the sword coming upon the land, if he blows the **trumpet** and warns the people, then whoever hears the sound of the **trumpet** and does not take warning, if the sword comes and takes him away, his blood shall be on his own head. He heard the sound of the **trumpet**, but did not take warning; his blood shall be upon himself. But he who takes warning will save his life. But if the watchman sees the sword coming and does not blow the **trumpet**, and the people are not warned, and the sword comes and takes any person from among them, he is taken away in his iniquity; but his blood I will require at the watchman's hand.'

Hosea 5:8 (2 references—ram's horn and trumpet): "Blow the **ram's horn** in Gibeah, The **trumpet** in Ramah! Cry aloud at Beth Aven, 'Look behind you, O Benjamin!'

Hosea 8:1: Set the **trumpet** to your mouth! He shall come like an eagle against the house of the LORD, Because they have transgressed My covenant and rebelled against My law.

Joel 2:1: Blow the **trumpet** in Zion, and sound an alarm in My holy mountain! Let all the inhabitants of the land tremble; for the day of the LORD is coming, for it is at hand:

Joel 2:15: Blow the **trumpet** in Zion, consecrate a fast, call a sacred assembly;

Amos 2:2: But I will send a fire upon Moab, And it shall devour the palaces of Kerioth; Moab shall die with tumult, with shouting and **trumpet** sound.

Amos 3:6: If a **trumpet** is blown in a city, will not the people be afraid? If there is calamity in a city, will not the LORD have done it?

Zephaniah 1:16: A day of **trumpet** and alarm against the fortified cities and against the high towers.

Zechariah 9:14**: Then the LORD will be seen over them, and His arrow will go forth like lightning. The LORD God will blow the **trumpet**, and go with whirlwinds from the south.

Matthew 6:2: *Therefore, when you do a charitable deed, do not sound a **trumpet** before you as the hypocrites do in the synagogues and in the streets, that they may have glory from men. Assuredly, I say to you, they have their reward.*

Matthew 24:31: *And He will send His angels with a great sound of a **trumpet**, and they will gather together His elect from the four winds, from one end of heaven to the other.*

I Corinthians 14:8: *For if the **trumpet** makes an uncertain sound, who will prepare himself for battle?*

I Corinthians 15:52 *(2 references): in a moment, in the twinkling of an eye, at the last **trumpet**. For the **trumpet** will sound, and the dead will be raised incorruptible, and we shall be changed.*

I Thessalonians 4:16**: *For the Lord Himself will descend from heaven with a shout, with the voice of an archangel, and with the **trumpet** of God. And the dead in Messiah will rise first.*

Hebrews 12:19: *and the sound of a **trumpet** and the voice of words, so that those who heard it begged that the word should not be spoken to them anymore.*

Revelation 1:10**: *I was in the Spirit on the Lord's Day, and I heard behind me a loud voice, as of a **trumpet**,*

Revelation 4:1**: *After these things I looked, and behold, a door standing open in heaven. And the first voice which I heard was like a **trumpet** speaking with me, saying, 'Come up here, and I will show you things which must take place after this.'*

Revelation 8:7, 8 *(2 references—a trumpet): The first angel sounded (a **trumpet**): And hail and fire followed, mingled with blood, and they were thrown to the earth. And a third of the trees were burned up, and all green grass was burned up. Then the second angel sounded (a **trumpet**): And something like a great mountain burning with fire was thrown into the sea, and a third of the sea became blood.*

Revelation 8:10: *Then the third angel sounded (a **trumpet**): and a great star fell from heaven, burning like a torch, and it fell on a third of the rivers and on the springs of water.*

Revelation 8:12, 13 *(2 references—a trumpet and trumpet): Then the fourth angel sounded (a **trumpet**): And a third of the sun was struck, a third of the moon, and a third of the stars, so that a third of them were* *darkened. A third of the day did not shine, and likewise the night. And I looked, and I heard an angel flying through the midst of heaven, saying with a loud voice, "Woe, woe, woe to the inhabitants of the earth, because of the remaining blasts of the* **trumpet** *of the three angels who are about to sound!"*

Revelation 9:1: *Then the fifth angel sounded (a* **trumpet***): And I saw a star fallen from heaven to the earth. To him was given the key to the bottomless pit.*

Revelation 9:13, 14 *(2 references—a trumpet and trumpet): Then the sixth angel sounded (a* **trumpet***): And I heard a voice from the four horns of the golden altar which is before God, saying to the sixth angel who had the* **trumpet***, "Release the four angels who are bound at the great river Euphrates."*

Revelation 11:15: *Then the seventh angel sounded (a* **trumpet***): And there were loud voices in heaven, saying, 'The kingdoms of this world have become the kingdoms of our Lord and of His Messiah, and He shall reign forever and ever!"*

Ba'al Tekiah (Master Blowers—Trumpeters)

II Kings 11:14 *(2 references—trumpeters and trumpets): When she looked, there was the king standing by a pillar according to custom; and the leaders and the* **trumpeters** *were by the king. All the people of the land were rejoicing and blowing* **trumpets***. So Athaliah tore her clothes and cried out, "Treason! Treason!"*

II Chronicles 5:13 *(2 references—trumpeters and trumpets): indeed it came to pass, when the* **trumpeters** *and singers were as one, to make one sound to be heard in praising and thanking the LORD, and when they lifted up their voice with the* **trumpets** *and cymbals and instruments of music, and praised the LORD, saying: "For He is good, for His mercy endures forever," that the house, the house of the LORD, was filled with a cloud,*

II Chronicles 23:13 *(2 references—trumpeters and trumpets): When she looked, there was the king standing by his pillar at the entrance; and the leaders and the* **trumpeters** *were by the king. All the people of the land were rejoicing and blowing* **trumpets***, also the singers with musical instruments, and those who led in praise. So Athaliah tore her clothes and said, "Treason! Treason!"*

II Chronicles 29:28: *So all the assembly worshiped, the singers sang, and the* **trumpeters** *sounded; all this continued until the burnt offering was finished.*

Revelation 18:22: *The sound of harpists, musicians, flutists, and* ***trumpeters*** *shall not be heard in you anymore. No craftsman of any craft shall be found in you anymore, and the sound of a millstone shall not be heard in you anymore.*

Shofarot (Trumpets)

Leviticus 23:24: *"Speak to the children of Israel, saying: 'In the seventh month, on the first day of the month, you shall have a sabbath rest, a memorial of blowing of* ***trumpets****, a holy convocation.*

Numbers 10:2: *"Make two silver* ***trumpets*** *for yourself; you shall make them of hammered work; you shall use them for calling the congregation and for directing the movement of the camps.*

Numbers 10:8, 9, 10 *(3 references): The sons of Aaron, the priests, shall blow the* ***trumpets****; and these shall be to you as an ordinance forever throughout your generations. When you go to war in your land against the enemy who oppresses you, then you shall sound an alarm with the* ***trumpets****, and you will be remembered before the LORD your God, and you will be saved from your enemies. Also in the day of your gladness, in your appointed feasts, and at the beginning of your months, you shall blow the* ***trumpets*** *over your burnt offerings and over the sacrifices of your peace offerings; and they shall be a memorial for you before your God: I am the LORD your God.'*

Numbers 29:1: *'And in the seventh month, on the first day of the month, you shall have a holy convocation. You shall do no customary work. For you it is a day of blowing the* ***trumpets****.*

Numbers 31:6: *Then Moses sent them to the war, one thousand from each tribe; he sent them to the war with Phinehas the son of Eleazar the priest, with the holy articles and the signal* ***trumpets*** *in his hand.*

Joshua 6:4 *(2 references - trumpets of ram's horns and trumpets): And seven priests shall bear seven* ***trumpets*** *of* ***rams' horns*** *before the ark. But the seventh day you shall march around the city seven times, and the priests shall blow the* ***trumpets****.*

Joshua 6:6: *Then Joshua the son of Nun called the priests and said to them, "Take up the ark of the covenant, and let seven priests bear seven* ***trumpets*** *of* ***rams' horns*** *before the ark of the LORD.'*

Joshua 6:8, 9 *(4 references—trumpets of ram's horns and trumpets): So it was, when Joshua had spoken to the people, that the seven priests bearing the seven* ***trumpets*** *of* ***ram's horns*** *before the LORD advanced and blew the* ***trumpets****, and the ark of the covenant of the LORD followed them. The* *armed men went before the priests who blew the* **trumpets***, and the rear guard came after the ark, while the priests continued blowing the* **trumpets***.*

Joshua 6:13 *(3 references—trumpets of ram's horns and trumpets): Then seven priests bearing seven* **trumpets** *of* **ram's horns** *before the ark of the LORD went on continually and blew with the* **trumpets***. And the armed men went before them. But the rear guard came after the ark of the LORD, while the priests continued blowing the* **trumpets***.*

Joshua 6:16: *And the seventh time it happened, when the priests blew the* **trumpets***, that Joshua said to the people: 'Shout, for the LORD has given you the city!*

Joshua 6:20 *(2 references—trumpets and trumpet): So the people shouted when the priests blew the* **trumpets***. And it happened when the people heard the sound of the* **trumpet***, and the people shouted with a great shout, that the wall fell down flat. Then the people went up into the city, every man straight before him, and they took the city.*

Judges 7:8: *So the people took provisions and their* **trumpets** *in their hands. And he sent away all the rest of Israel, every man to his tent, and retained those three hundred men. Now the camp of Midian was below him in the valley.*

Judges 7:18, 19, 20: *When I blow the* **trumpets***, I and all who are with me, then you also blow the* **trumpets** *on every side of the whole camp, and say, 'The sword of the LORD and of Gideon!' So Gideon and the hundred men who were with him came to the outpost of the camp at the beginning of the middle watch, just as they had posted the watch; and they blew the* **trumpets** *and broke the pitchers that were in their hands. Then the three companies blew the* **trumpets** *and broke the pitchers—they held the torches in their left hands and the* **trumpets** *in their right hands for blowing—and they cried, "The sword of the LORD and of Gideon!"*

Judges 7:22: *When the three hundred blew the* **trumpets***, the LORD set every man's sword against his companion throughout the whole camp; and the army fled to Beth Acacia, toward Zererah, as far as the border of Abel Meholah, by Tabbath.*

II Kings 9:13: *Then each man hastened to take his garment and put it under him on the top of the steps; and they blew* **trumpets***, saying, "Jehu is king!"*

II Kings 12:13: *However there were not made for the house of the LORD basins of silver, trimmers, sprinkling-bowls,* **trumpets***, any articles of gold or articles of silver, from the money brought into the house of the LORD.*

I Chronicles 13:8: Then David and all Israel played music before God with all their might, with singing, on harps, on stringed instruments, on tambourines, on cymbals, and with **trumpets**.

I Chronicles 15:24: Shebaniah, Joshaphat, Nethanel, Amasai, Zechariah, Benaiah, and Eliezer, the priests, were to blow the **trumpets** before the ark of God; and Obed-Edom and Jehiah, doorkeepers for the ark.

I Chronicles 15:28: Thus all Israel brought up the ark of the covenant of the LORD with shouting and with the sound of the horn, with **trumpets** and with cymbals, making music with stringed instruments and harps.

I Chronicles 16:6: Benaiah and Jahaziel the priests regularly blew the **trumpets** before the ark of the covenant of God.

I Chronicles 16:42: and with them Heman and Jeduthun, to sound aloud with **trumpets** and cymbals and the musical instruments of God. Now the sons of Jeduthun were gatekeepers.

II Chronicles 5:12: and the Levites who were the singers, all those of Asaph and Heman and Jeduthun, with their sons and their brethren, stood at the east end of the altar, clothed in white linen, having cymbals, stringed instruments and harps, and with them one hundred and twenty priests sounding with **trumpets**

II Chronicles 7:6: And the priests attended to their services; the Levites also with instruments of the music of the LORD, which King David had made to praise the LORD, saying, "For His mercy endures forever," whenever David offered praise by their ministry. The priests sounded **trumpets** opposite them, while all Israel stood.

II Chronicles 13:12: "Now look, God Himself is with us as our head, and His priests with sounding **trumpets** to sound the alarm against you. O children of Israel, do not fight against the LORD God of your fathers, for you shall not prosper!"

II Chronicles 13:14: And when Judah looked around, to their surprise the battle line was at both front and rear; and they cried out to the LORD, and the priests sounded the **trumpets**.

II Chronicles 15:14 (2 references—trumpets and ram's horns): Then they took an oath before the LORD with a loud voice, with shouting and **trumpets** and **ram's horns**.

II Chronicles 20:28: So they came to Jerusalem, with stringed instruments and harps and **trumpets**, to the house of the LORD.

II Chronicles 29:26,27 *(2 references—trumpets): The Levites stood with the instruments of David, and the priests with the* **trumpets**. *Then Hezekiah commanded them to offer the burnt offering on the altar. And when the burnt offering began, the song of the LORD also began, with the* **trumpets** *and with the instruments of David king of Israel.*

Ezra 3:10: *When the builders laid the foundation of the temple of the LORD, the priests stood in their apparel with* **trumpets**, *and the Levites, the sons of Asaph, with cymbals, to praise the LORD, according to the ordinance of David king of Israel.*

Nehemiah 12:35: *and some of the priests' sons with* **trumpets**—*Zechariah the son of Jonathan, the son of Shemaiah, the son of Mattaniah, the son of Michaiah, the son of Zaccur, the son of Asaph,*

Nehemiah 12:41: *and the priests, Eliakim, Maaseiah, Minjamin, Michaiah, Elioenai, Zechariah, and Hananiah, with* **trumpets**;

Psalm 98:6 *(2 references—trumpets and horn): With* **trumpets** *and the sound of a* **horn**; *shout joyfully before the LORD, the King.*

Revelation 8:2: *And I saw the seven angels who stand before God, and to them were given seven* **trumpets**.

Revelation 8:6: *So the seven angels who had the seven* **trumpets** *prepared themselves to sound.*

Their faces I formed so that mine they would seek.

Ears to listen for the Word I would speak.

Eyes to see, minds to understand.

All they required I made with my Hand.

The Law and the Prophets for centuries foretold,

the birth of a baby begotten of old.

In words unencoded, with language so plain

that even the simplest could call on my Name.

Fathom mysteries confounding the wise,

see the Mashiach through a child's eyes.

The Messiah Revealed in the Hebrew Scriptures

Glimpse the dawn of a Son,	*Isaiah 9:6*
born of a virgin, the Anointed One.	*Isaiah 7:14*
Humblest of servants, child of the King,	*Isaiah 42:1*
the Righteous Branch	*Jeremiah 23:5*
and source of our healing.	*Isaiah 35:4-6*
Man of sorrows reviled and attacked,	*Isaiah 53:3*
riding in triumph on a donkey's back.	
Entering Jerusalem worshiped and praised	*Zechariah 9:9*
for pieces of silver then sold as a slave.	*Zechariah 11:12*
Blameless but beaten for crimes not his own,	*Isaiah 53:9-10*
hands and feet pierced yet no broken bone.	*Psalm 34:20*
Buried with rich men, he rose from the grave,	*Isaiah 53:9 & Psalm 16:9-10*
eternal High Priest, his people to save.	*Psalm 110:4*

    —by Jon Isaac

Your question should be, "Who is this Messiah that the Hebrew Scriptures were pointing to?"

The Book of Proverbs gives us a clue:

Proverbs 30:4:

> *"Who has gone up to heaven and come down? Who has cupped the wind in the palms of his hands? Who has wrapped up the waters in his cloak? Who established all the ends of the earth? What is his name, and what is his son's name? Surely you know!"*

If you know who He is, call out to Him and let Him be your Messiah, King and Redeemer. The world knows and God says that you know that Yeshua IS the Voice of God and your Redeemer! The Word of God gives clear evidence of this! The question is "Is He your Messiah—have you placed your trust in Yeshua HaMashiach (Yeshua the Messiah) and the sacrifice that He made on Calvary?" There is only one way to the Father, and that is through His Son. Just as the Israelites had to individually apply the "Blood of the Lamb" to the doorposts and lentils, we too must apply the "Blood of the Lamb" to our hearts so that we may receive our Salvation!

Yeshua has come once as Mashiach ben Joseph (the suffering servant) and he is just waiting on you to come again as Mashiach ben David (the conquering King).

Luke 13:34-35:

> *"O Jerusalem, Jerusalem, the one who kills the prophets and stones those who are sent to her! How often I wanted to gather your children together, as a hen gathers her brood under her wings, but you were not willing! See! Your house is left to you desolate; and assuredly, I say to you, you shall not see Me until the time comes when you say, "Blessed is He who comes in the name of the Lord!"'*

Whoever calls upon the name of the Lord shall be redeemed. Isn't it time that you called upon the name of the Lord?

Romans 10:1-13:

> *Brethren, my heart's desire and prayer to God for Israel is that they may be saved. For I bear them witness that they have a zeal for God, but not according to knowledge. For they being ignorant of God's righteousness, and seeking to establish their own righteousness, have not submitted to the righteousness of God.*

For Christ is the end of the law for righteousness to everyone who believes. For Moses writes about the righteousness which is of the law, "The man who does those things shall live by them: But the righteousness of faith speaks in this way, "Do not say in your heart, 'Who will ascend into heaven?'" (that is, to bring Christ down from above) or, "'Who will descend into the abyss?'" (that is, to bring Christ up from the dead). But what does it say? "The word is near you, in your mouth and in your heart"(that is, the word of faith which we preach): that if you confess with your mouth the Lord Yeshua and believe in your heart that God has raised Him from the dead, you will be saved.

For with the heart one believes unto righteousness, and with the mouth confession is made unto salvation. For the Scripture says, "Whoever believes on Him will not be put to shame." For there is no distinction between Jew and Greek, for the same Lord over all is rich to all who call upon Him. For "whoever calls on the name of the LORD shall be saved."

For the passage quoted says that "*everyone who rests his trust on him will not be humiliated.*" That means that there is no difference between Jew and Gentile in the eyes of the LORD. *ADONAI* is the same for everyone, rich toward everyone who calls on Him, since everyone who calls on the name of *ADONAI* will be delivered.

PRONUNCIATION FOR HEBREW TRANSLITERATIONS:

a	as in father
ai	as in aisle
ay	as in bay
e	as in send
ee	as in creed
o	as in pole
oo	as in boot
ch	as in loch

VOCABULARY:

ADONAI	The LORD
Aharon	Aaron
Avraham	Abraham
B.C.E.	Before the Common Era (B.C.)
Ben	son of
B'rit Chadeshah	Apostolic Writings of the Newer Covenant
C.E.	Common Era (A.D.)
Eliyahoo	Elijah
El Shaddai	God Almighty
Goyim	Gentiles
Haftarah	the Writings and the Prophets from the Older Covenant
HaGadol	the Great
Kefa	Peter

VOCABULARY: (Continued)

Messiah	Christ
Moshe	Moses
Ruach HaKodesh	Holy Spirit
Shabbat	Saturday or any Holy Convocation Day specified in Leviticus
Shofar	Ram's Horn or Trumpet
Talmadim	Disciples
Tanakh	Old Testament
Torah	The Five Books of Moses
Tziyon	Zion
Ya'akov	Jacob
Yah	God
Yerushalayim	Jerusalem
Yeshua	Yeshua
Yeshua HaMashiach	Yeshua the Messiah
Yitzchak	Isaac
Yochanan	John

Scripture taken from the New King James Version. Copyright © 1982 by Thomas Nelson,Inc. Used by permission. All rights reserved

Shofar - Yom Teruah, Jewish Outreach Institute, http://www.joi.org/celebrate/rosh/shofar.shtml

The Significance of the Shofar (Trumpet), Rivers in The Desert, https://www.flashfloods.com/home/about/shofar.html

The Shofar Users Manual, Daniel Bingamon, Jubilee Musical Inst. Co., http://www.bingamon.com/jubilee/shofar.htm

Sounding the Shofar, Jewish Magnes Museum, http://www.piney.com/Shofar.html

The Shofar, Living Emblems, Dr. John Garr, The Restoration Foundation, http://www.restorationfoundation.org

The Shofar, Encyclopedia - Judaica, CD Rom Edition

The New Strong's Exhaustive Concordance of the Bible (New Exhaustive Concordance of the Bible) by James Strong (Mar 2, 2010)

NOTES

NOTES

NOTES